Happy World of Paintings Vol. II

Author : Dr. Sudha Kumari

ISBN 13 : 978-1717034175

Copyright © Author

All rights reserved

Edited, book design and cover art by : Author

First Edition : March, 2017, India

Second Edition : May, 2018

Published and printed by : CreateSpace, USA

Reviews

"In an effort to uniformly portray the divine beauty of nature and of human heart, the artist ….displaying it in a unique way… shows her devotion to art maintained since her student days…Most of them in classical style…Every art lover was overwhelmed with an inexpressible joy at the sight of the paintings.."

-Asomiya Pratidin, popular daily, North-east India on release of 'Happy World of Paintings' during author's art exhibition under the same name.

"Author has displayed her artistic talent in the book (Happy World of Paintings).."

-Poorvanchal Prahari, popular daily, North-east India.

"Picturisation in a book form convenient way for art lovers to view the paintings.."

- Dainik Janmabhoomi, popular daily, North-east India.

"Exquisite beauty of nature has been displayed by her…"

- DY 365, popular TV channel, North-east India on exhibition of paintings and release of 'Happy World of Paintings'.

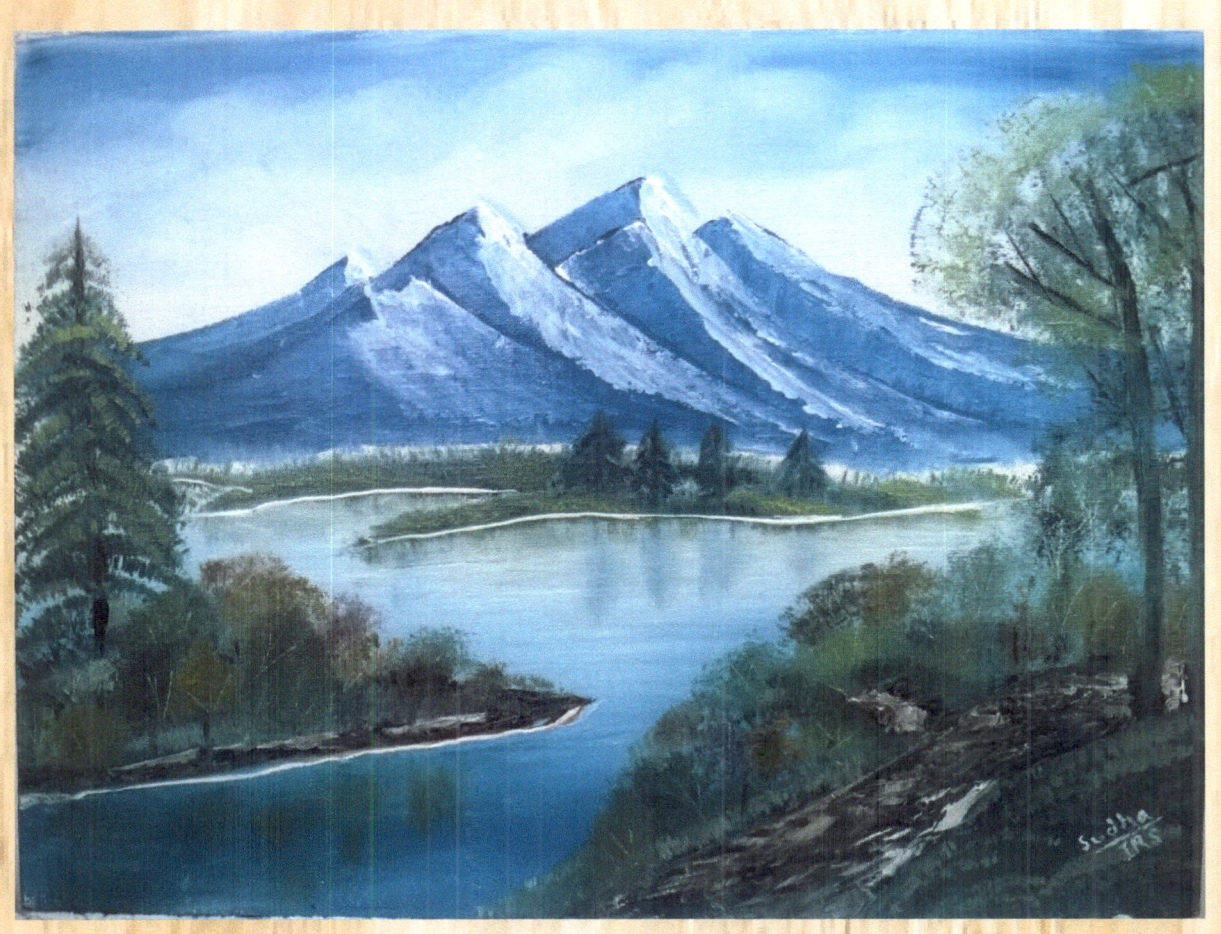

Morning over the Lake (oil) 2016

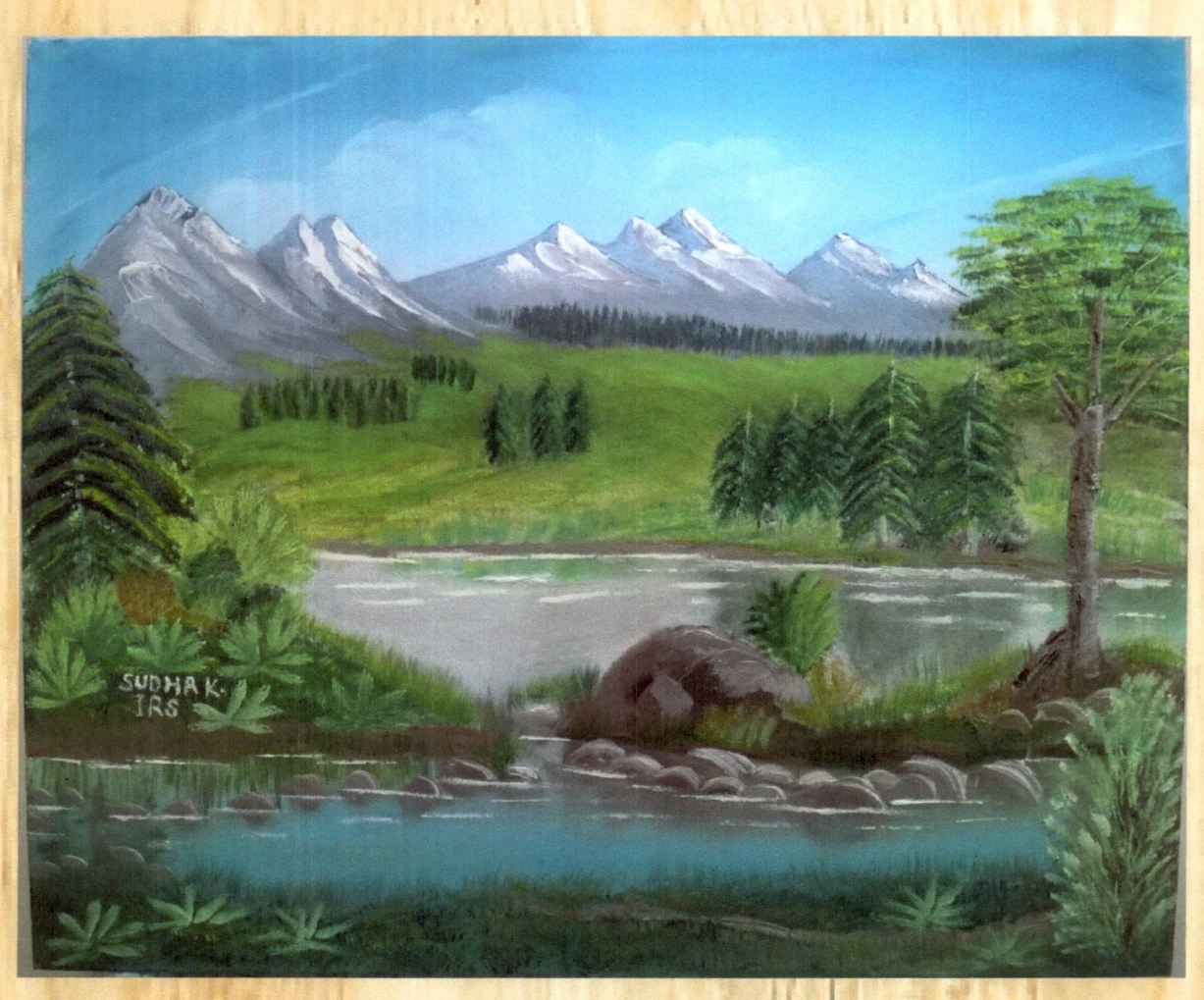

The Spring Season (oil) 2016

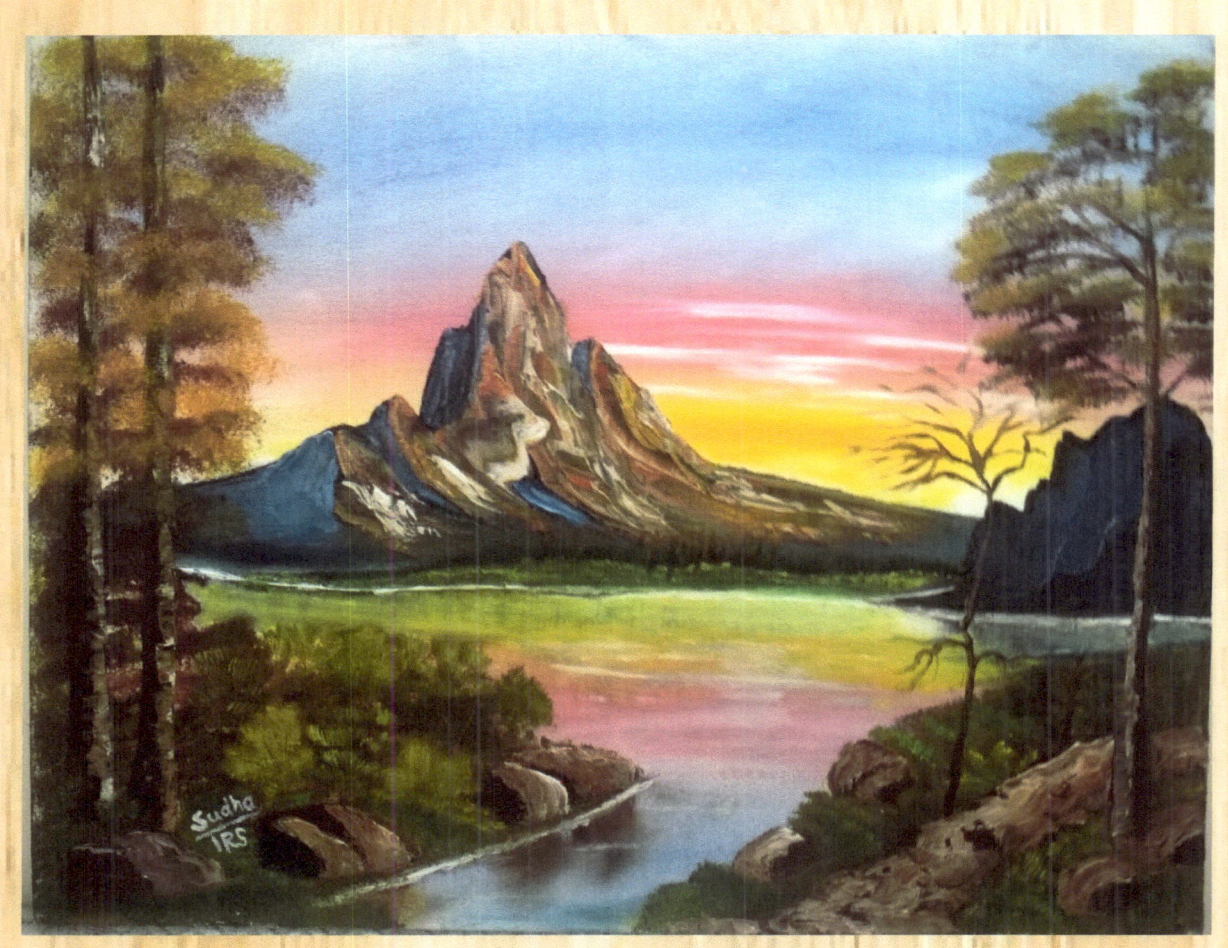

Sunset Lake (oil) 2016

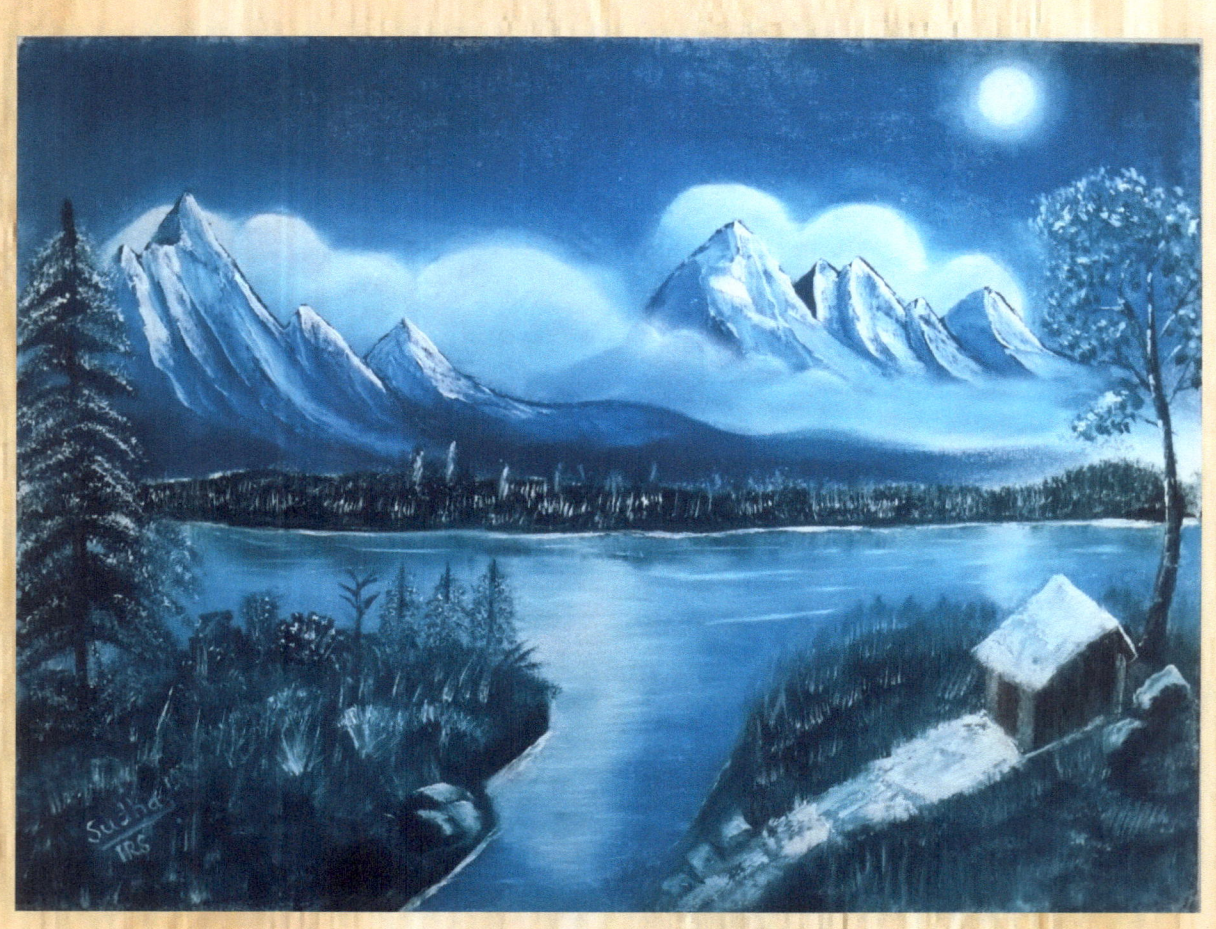

Winter Night (oil) 2016

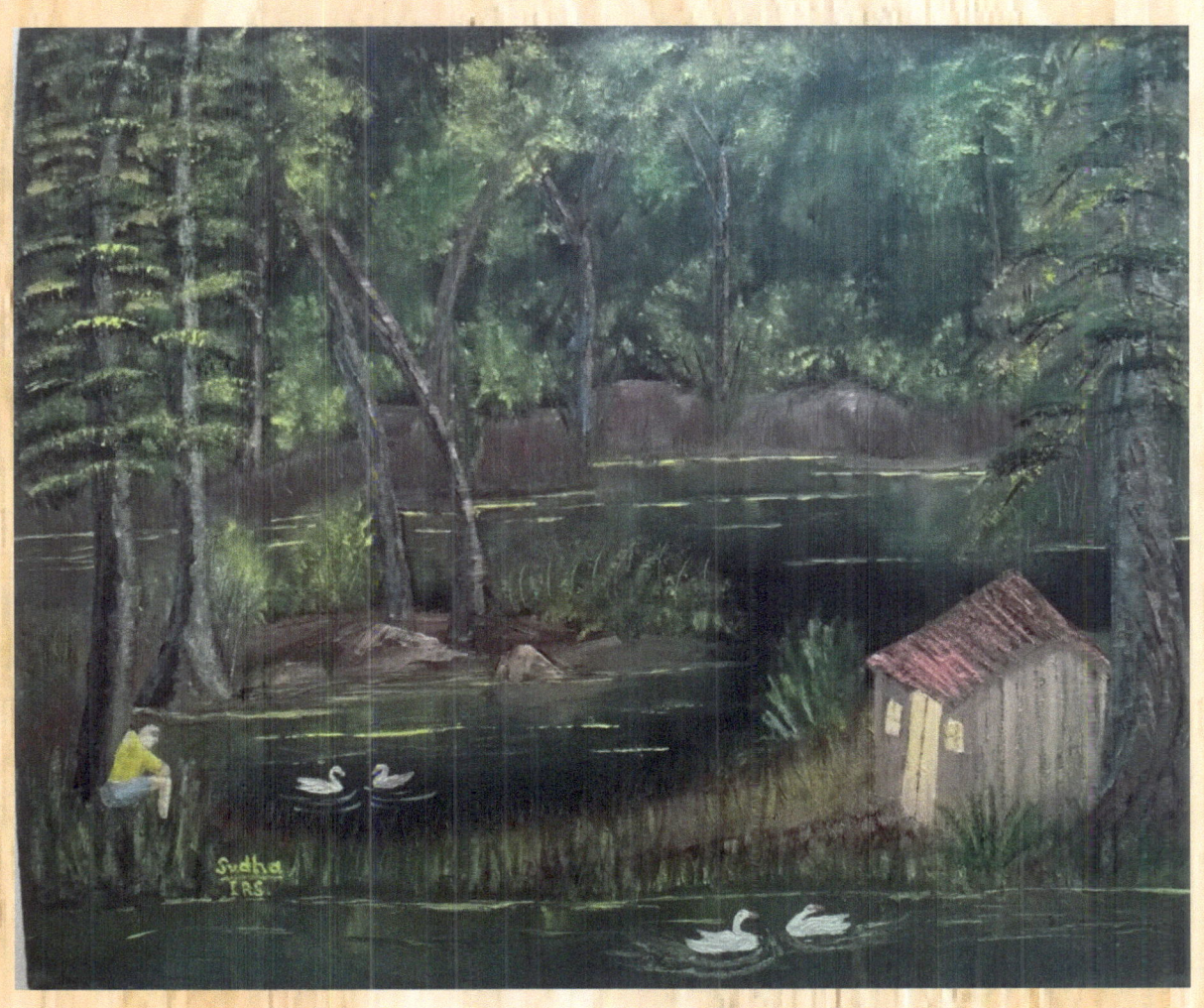

Boy at the Backwaters (oil) 2016

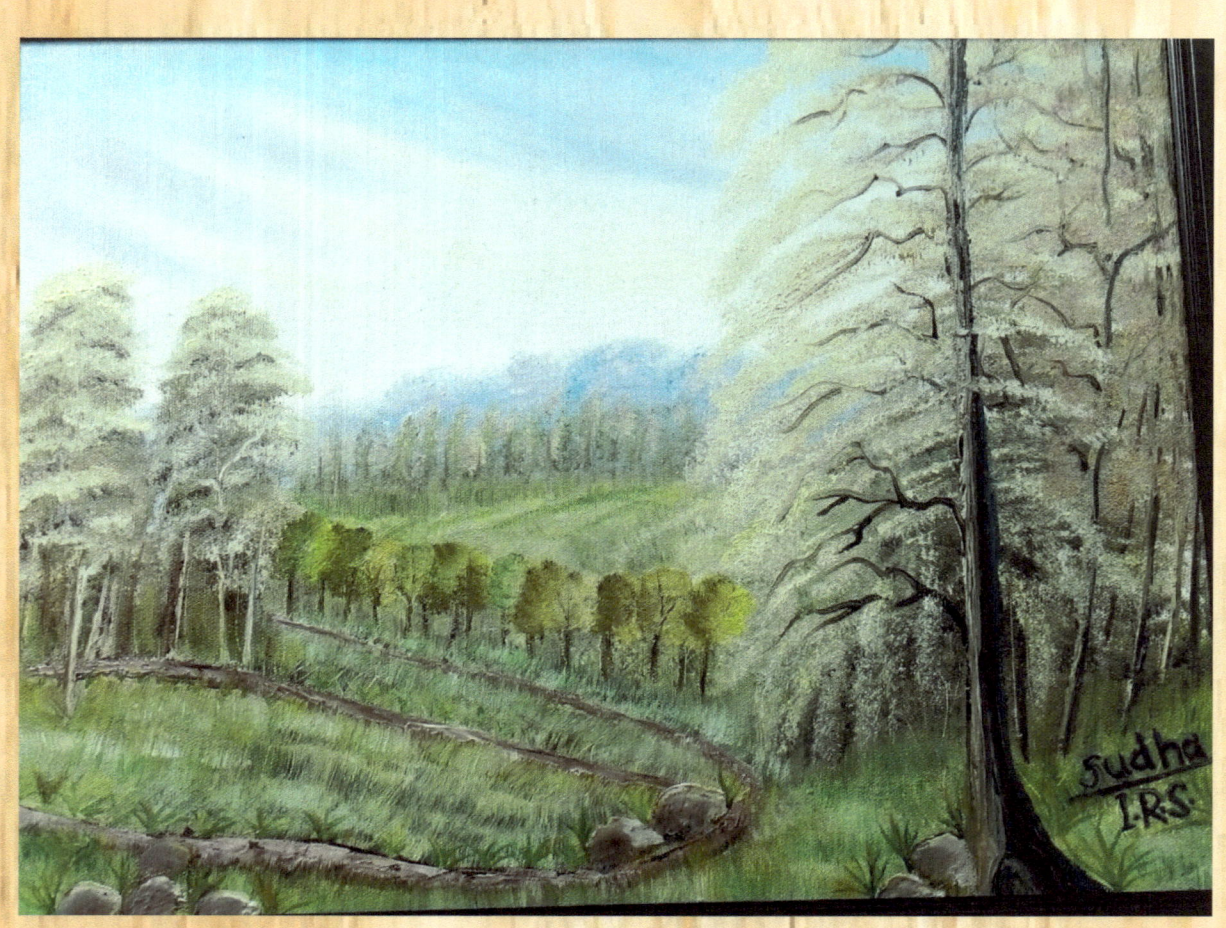

Golden Summer (oil) 2018

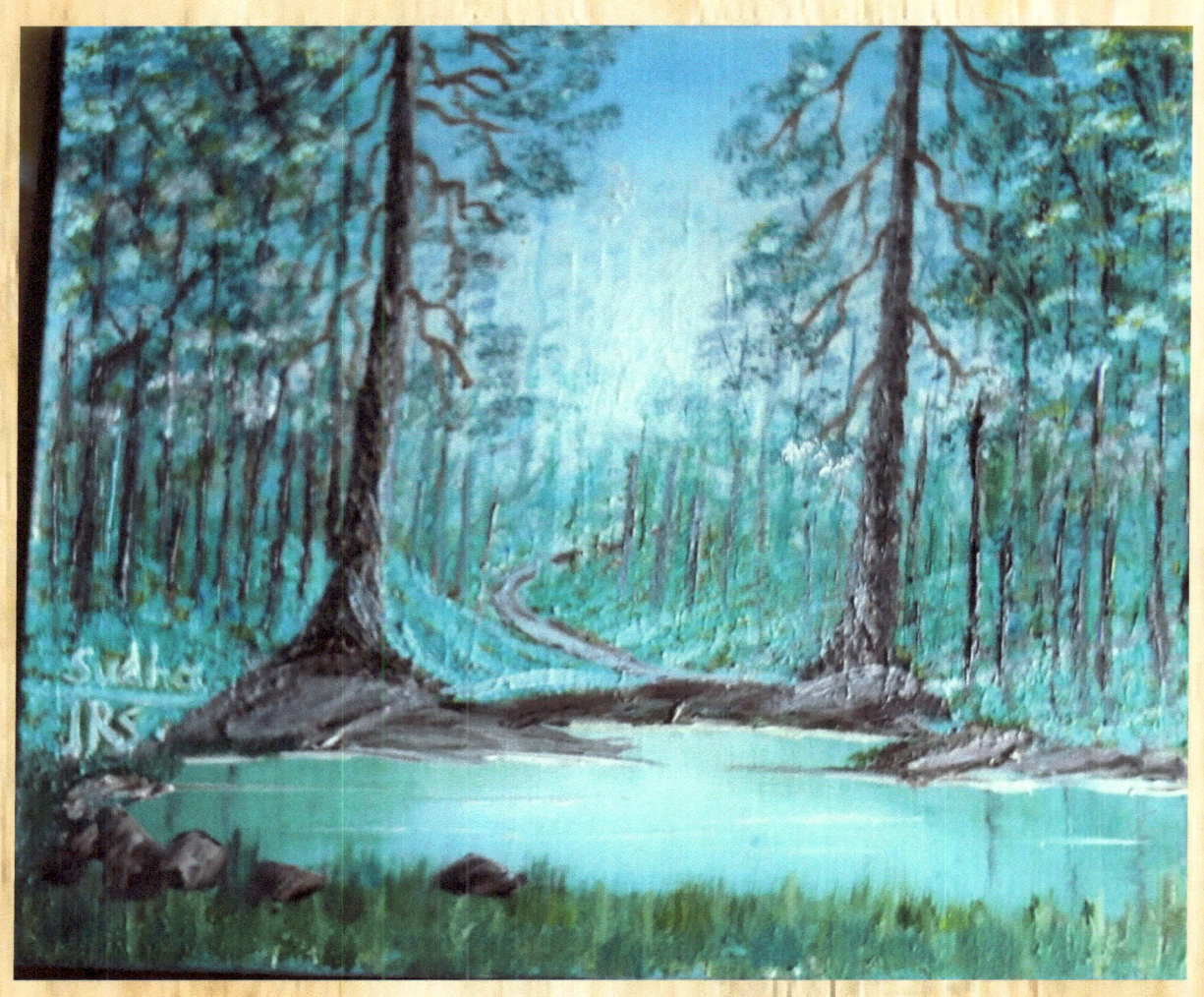

Woods are Lovely (oil) 2017

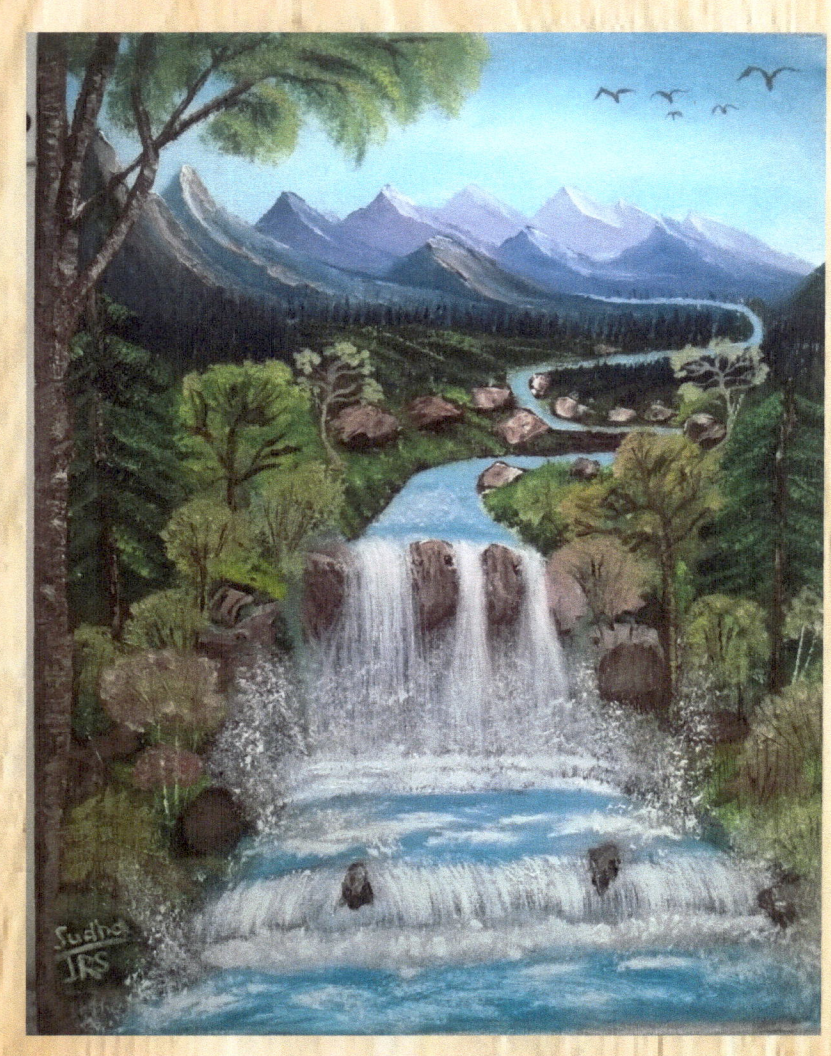

The Waterfall (oil) 2016

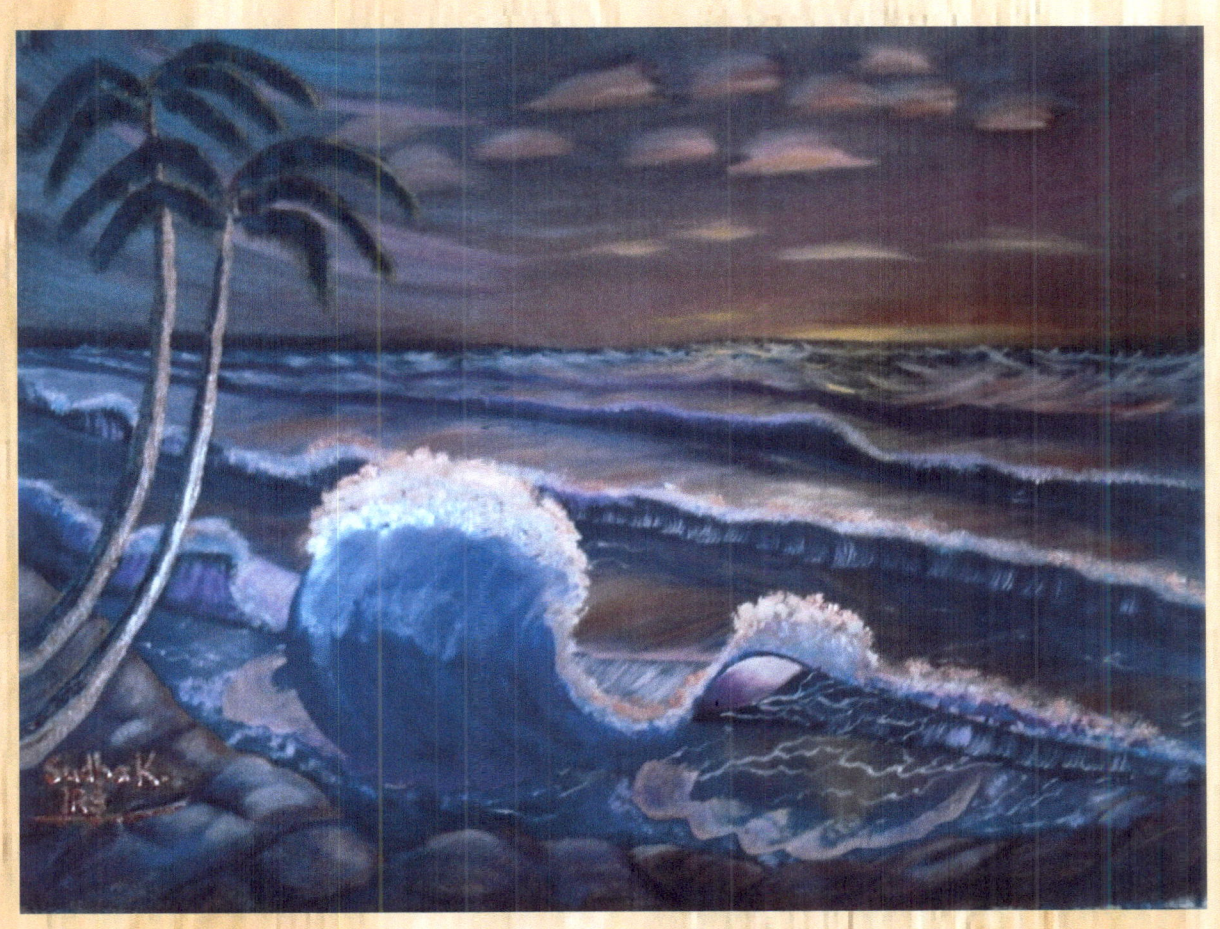

The Tide (oil) 2017

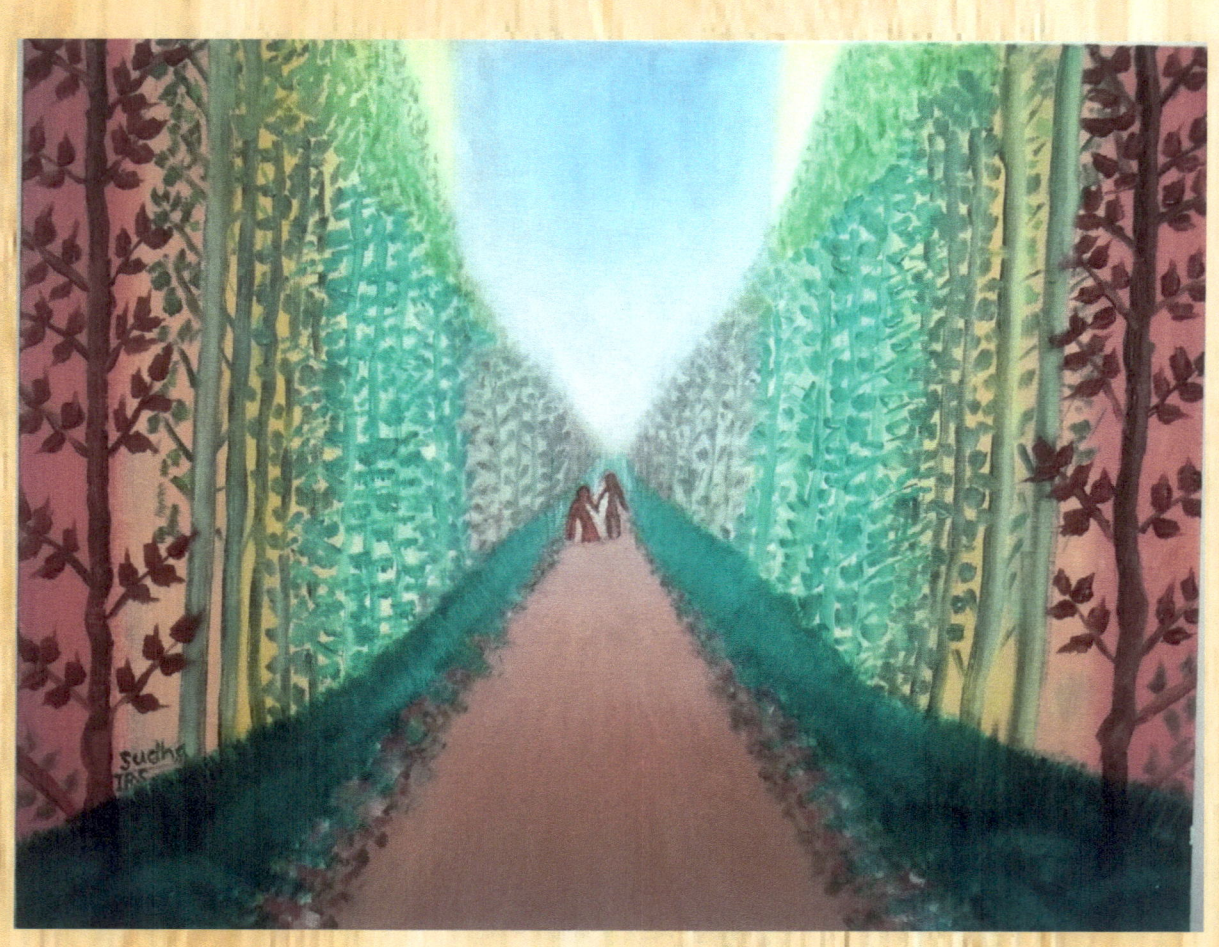

Companionship (oil) 2016

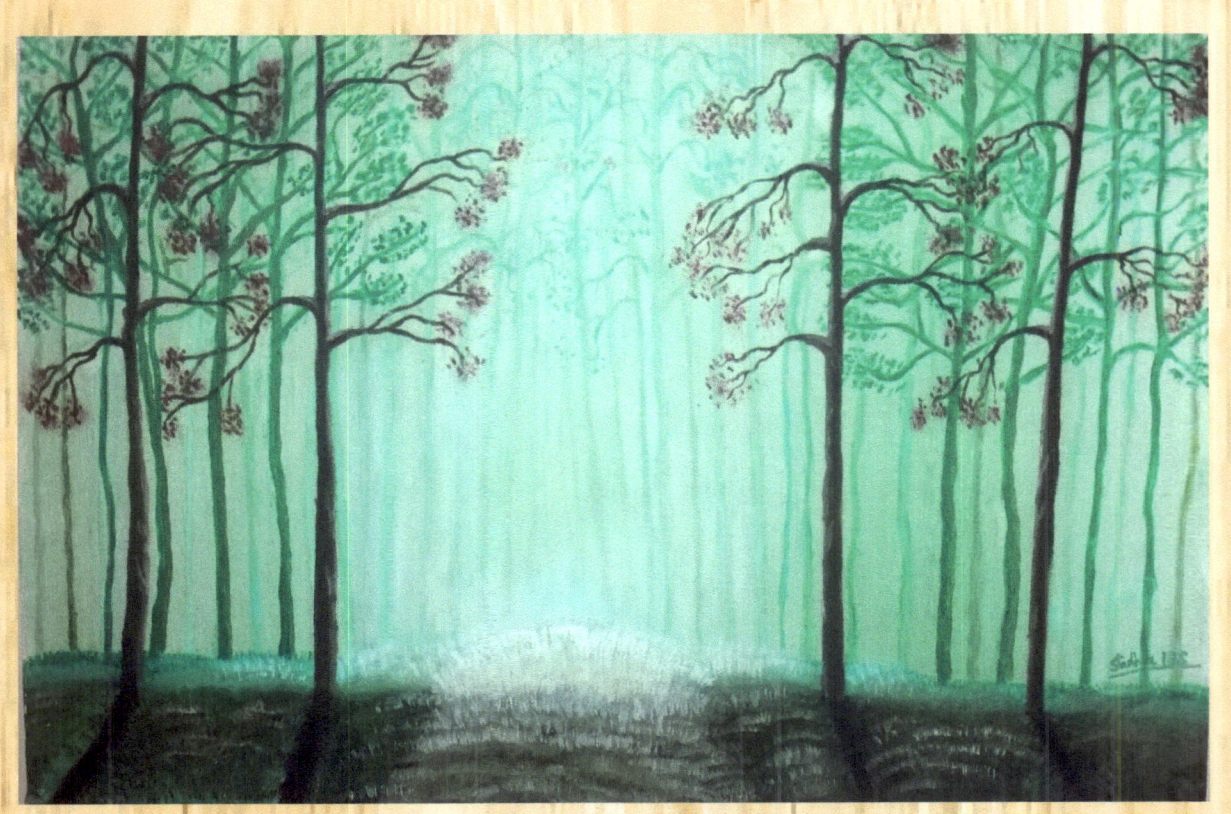

Forest (oil) 2016

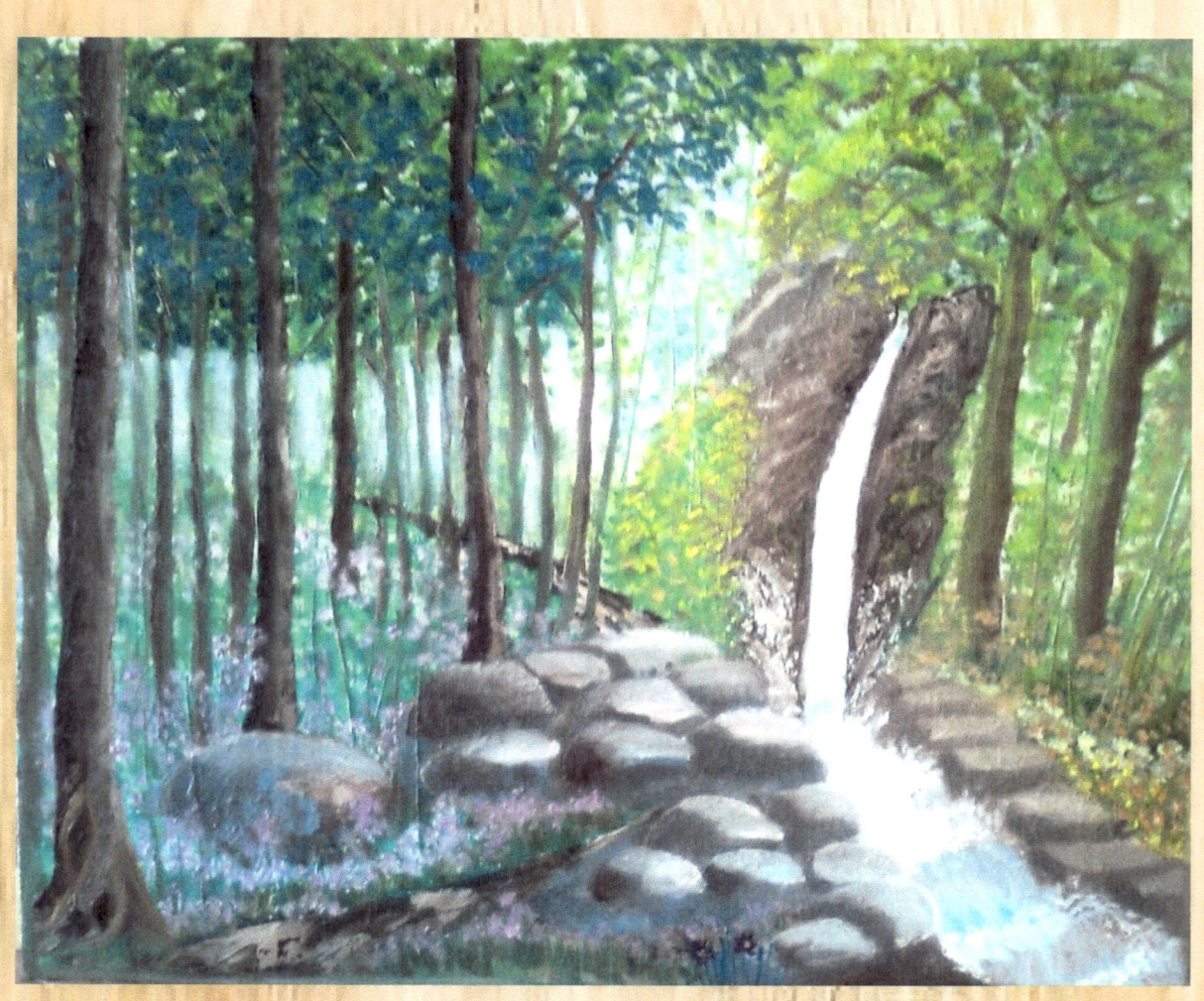

Hidden Fountain (oil) 2017

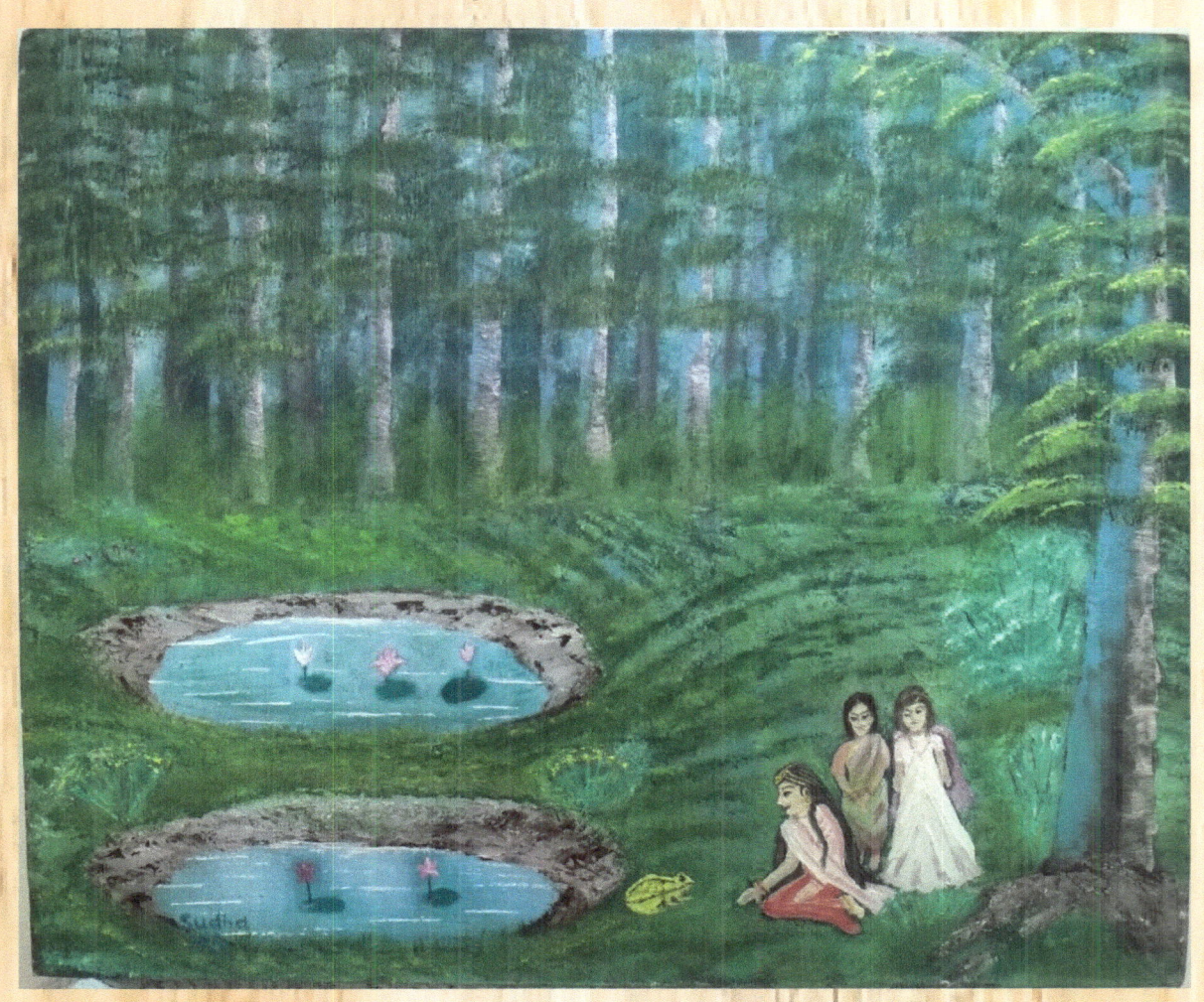

The Frog Prince (oil) 2016

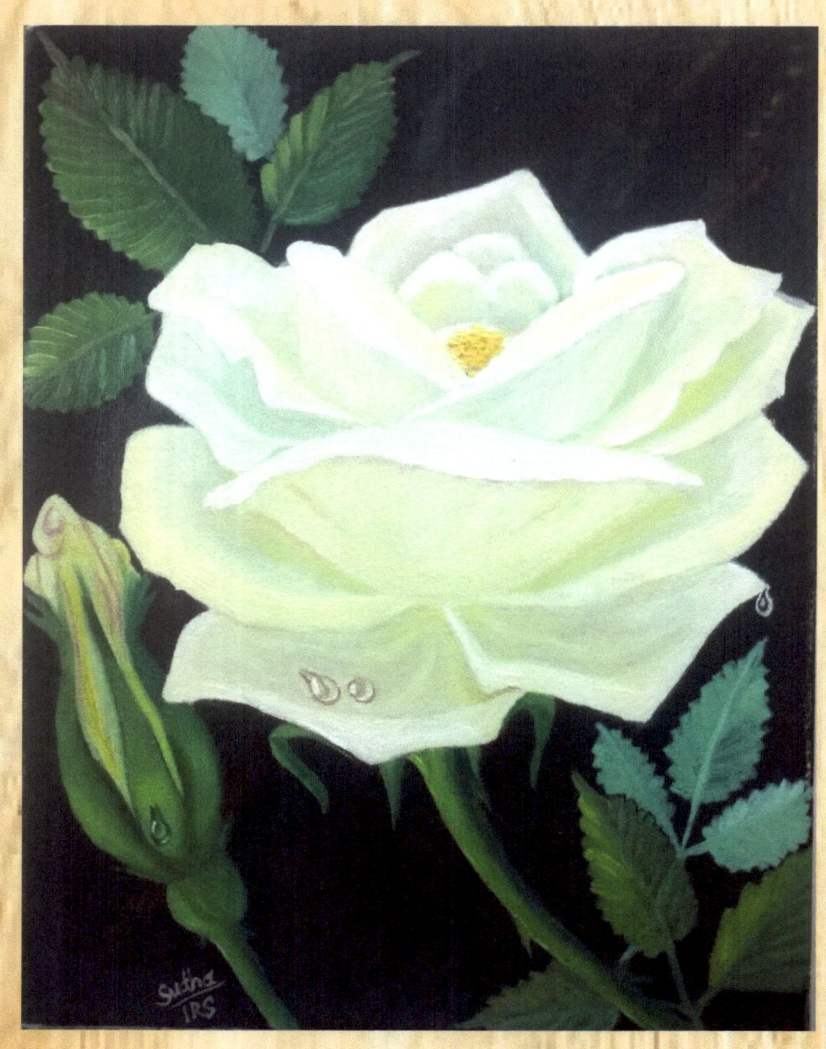

Yellow Rose (oil) 2016

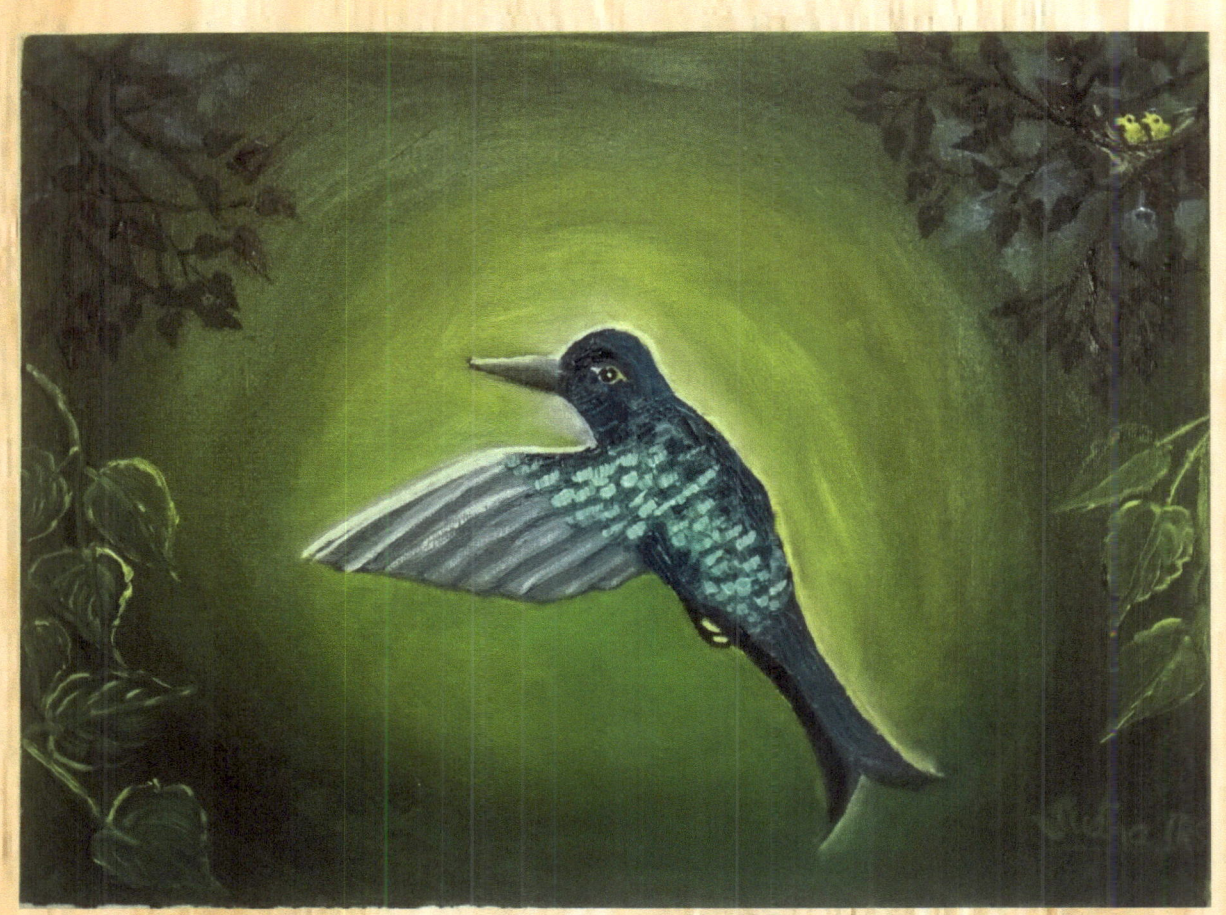

Blue Bird (oil) 2016

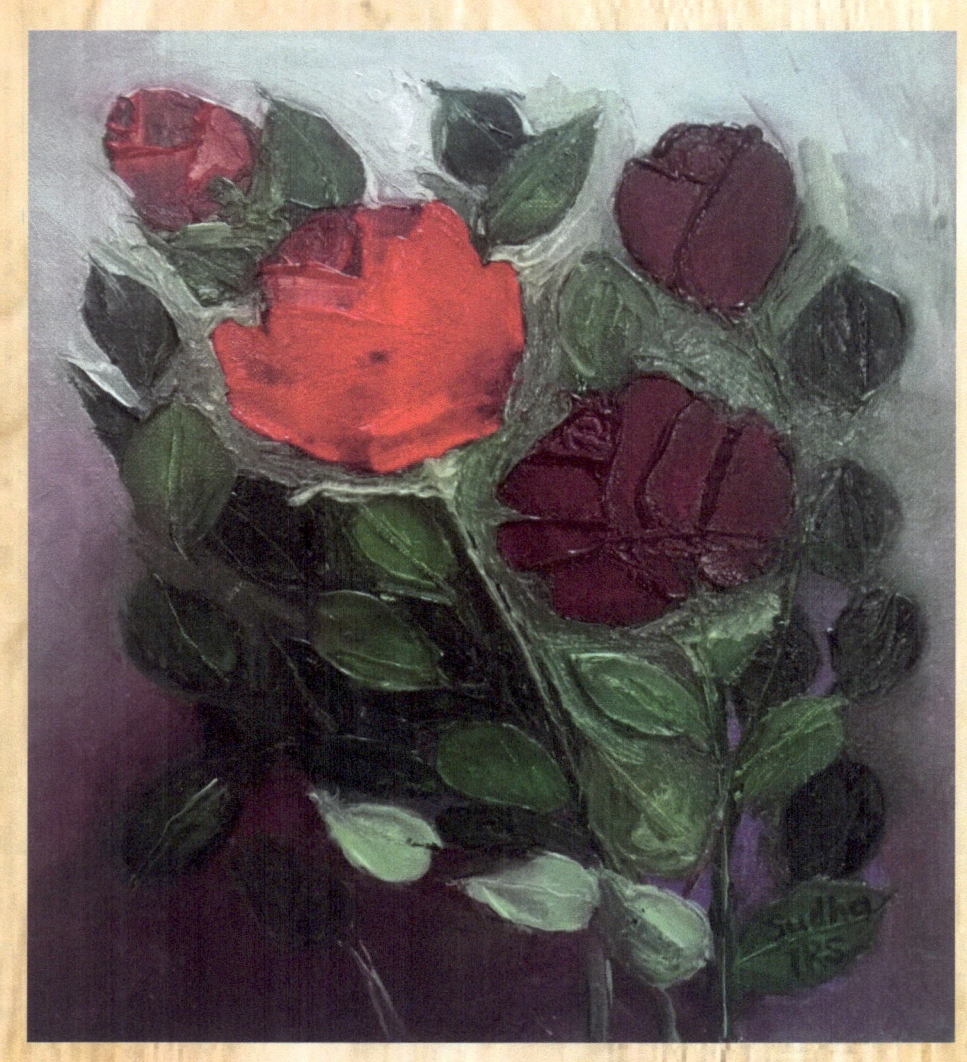

Crimson Rose (oil, palette knife) 2016

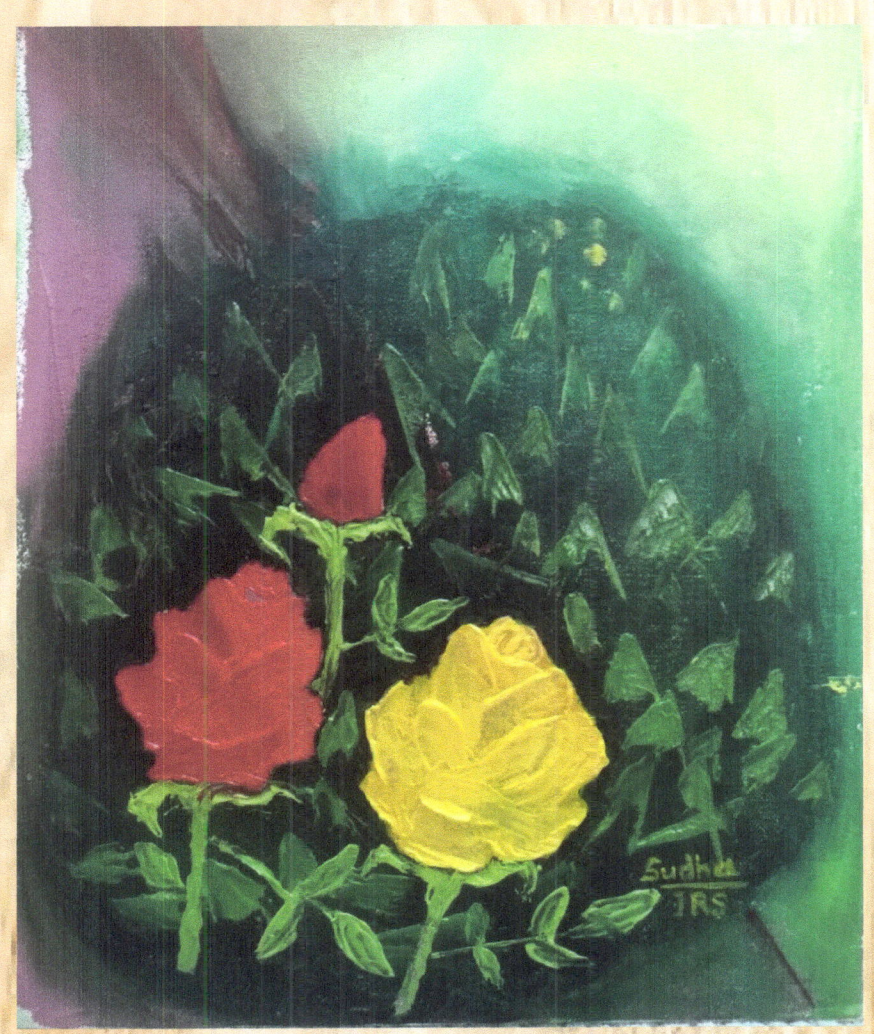

Red Rose (oil, palette knife) 2016

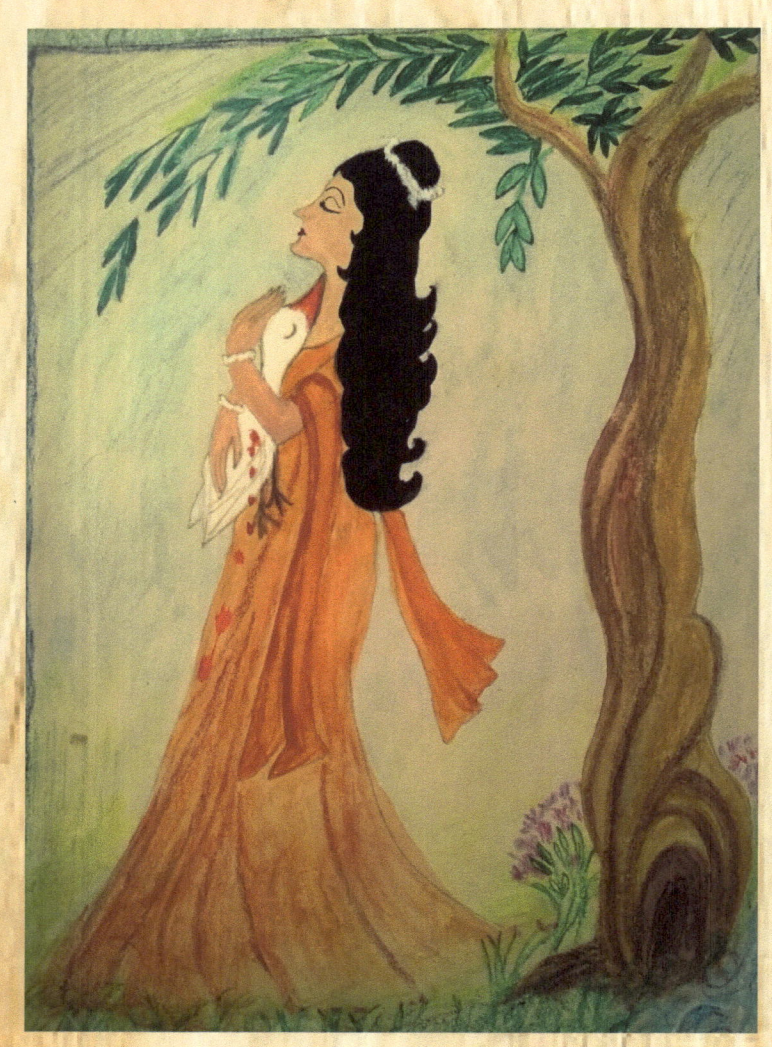

Compassion (water) 1980

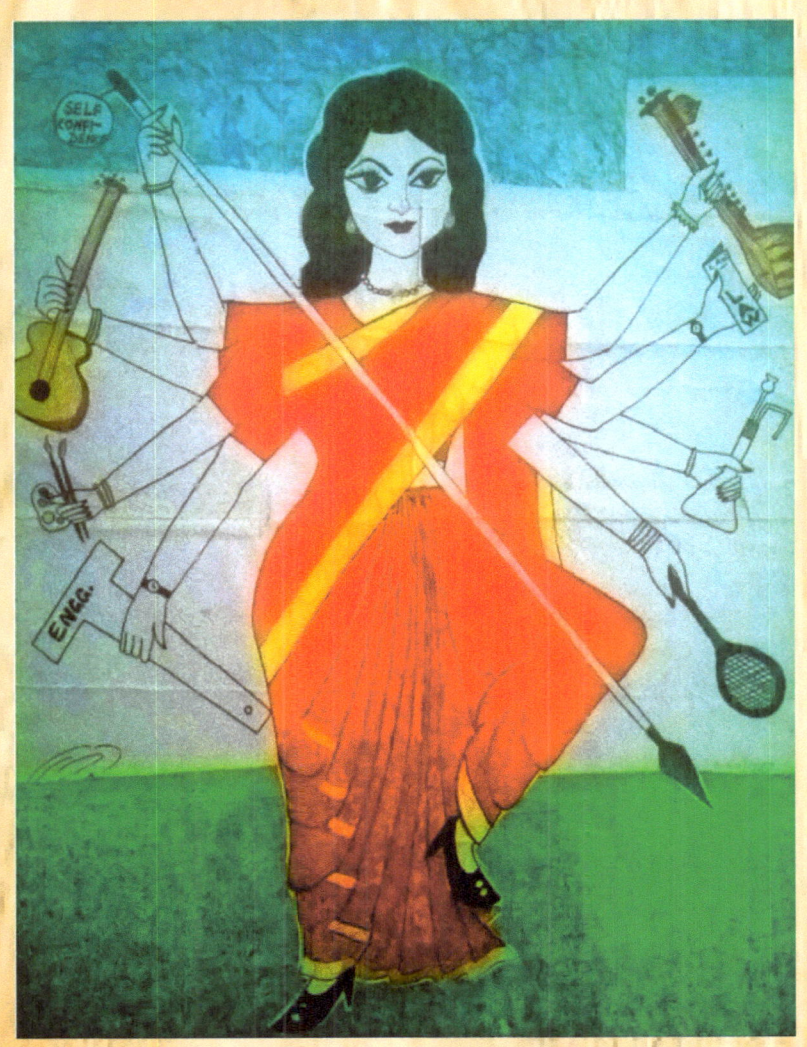

Beautiful Mind (water) 1986

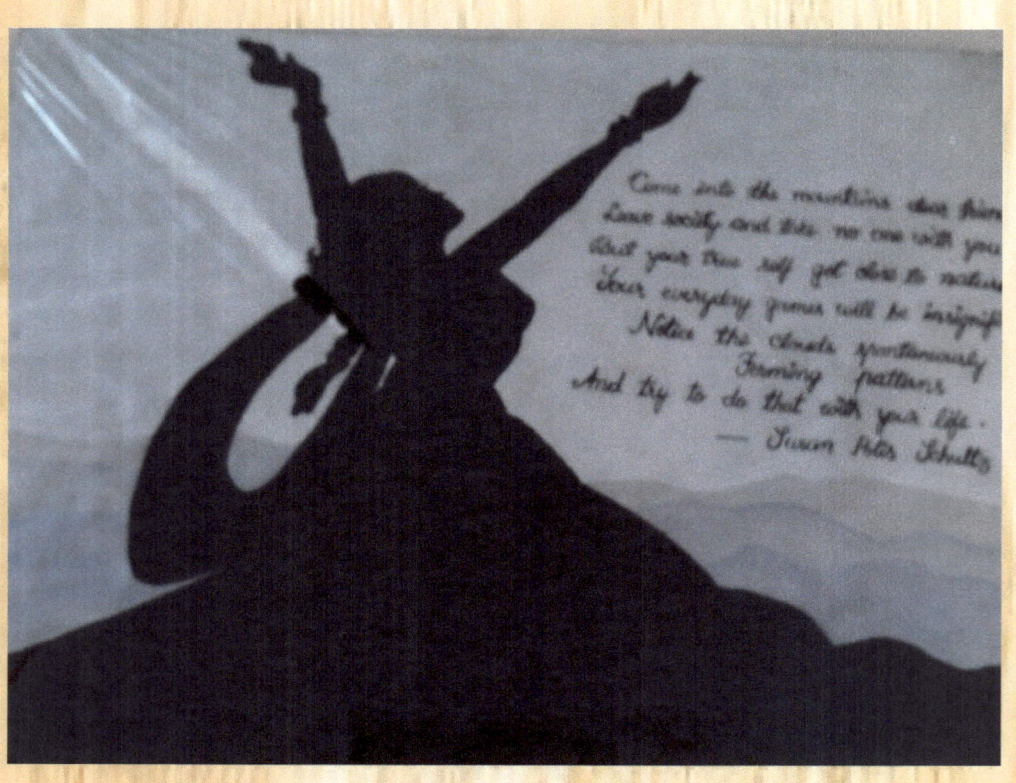

Heavens are listening ! (water), 1987

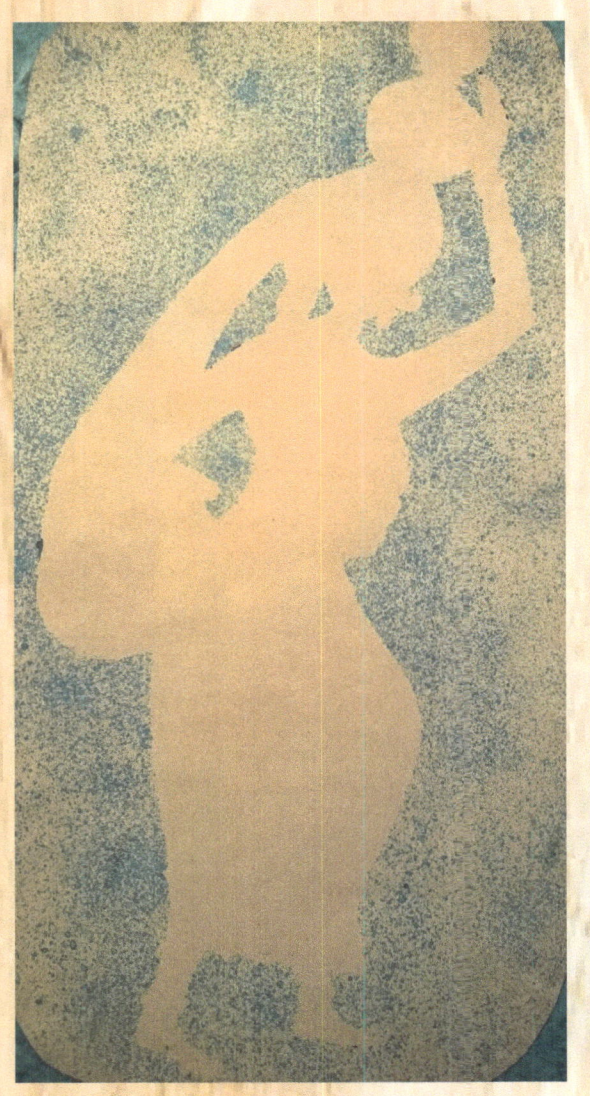
Spray Paint (water) 1977

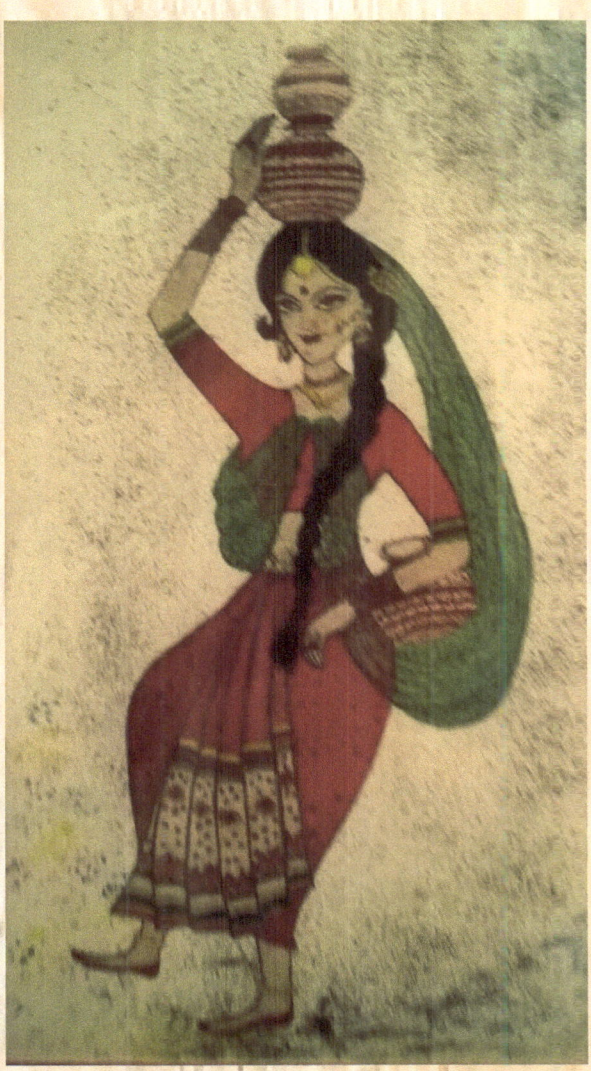
The Pitcher (water) 1977

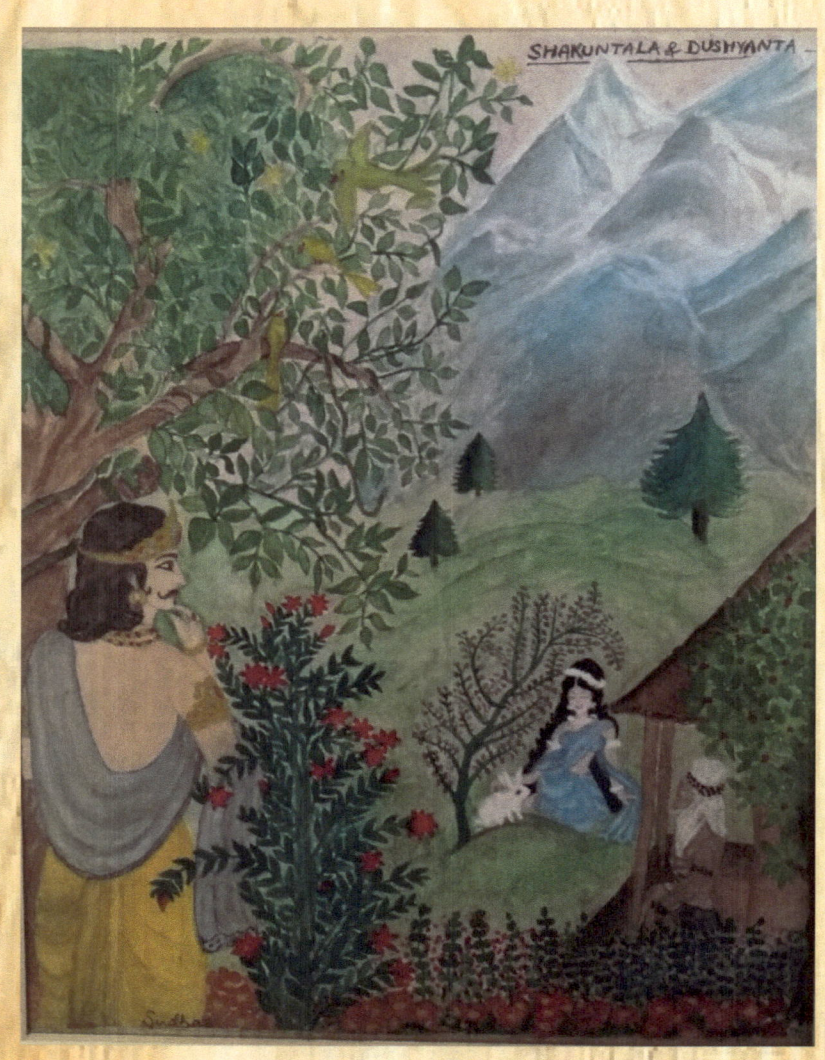

Shakuntala (water) 1978

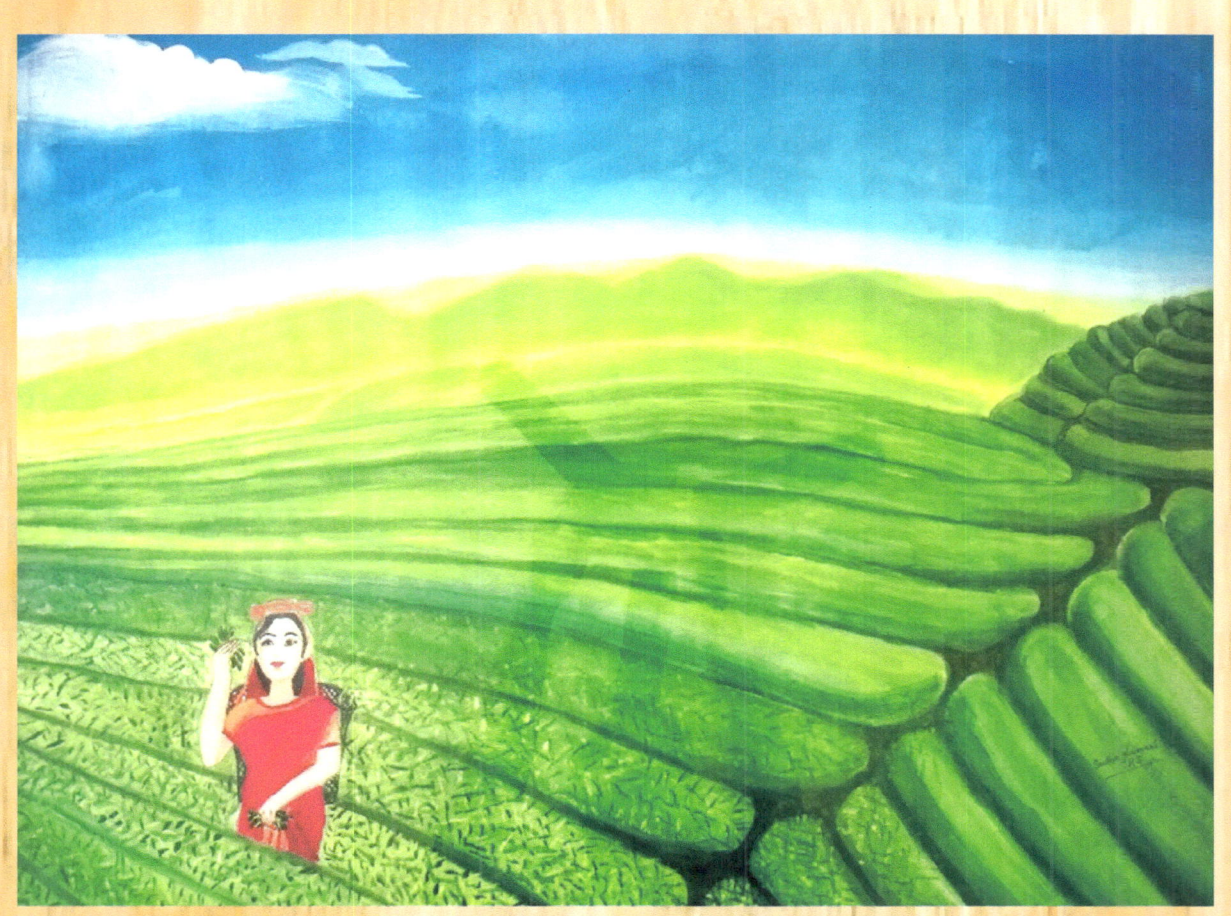

Tea Gardens (water) 2016

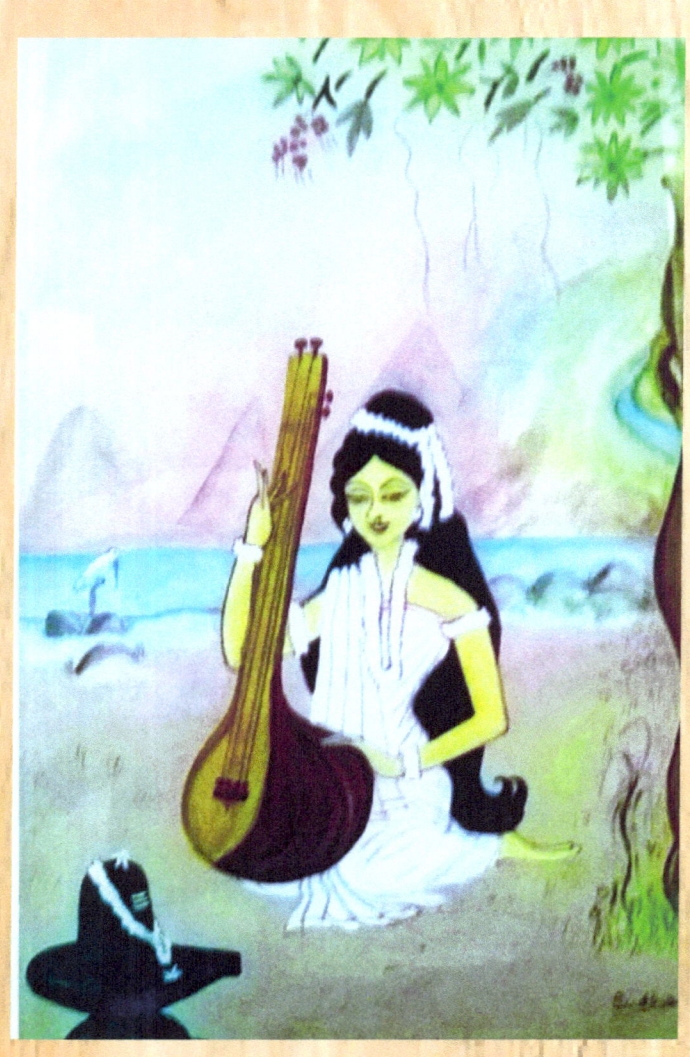

In Worship (water) 1977

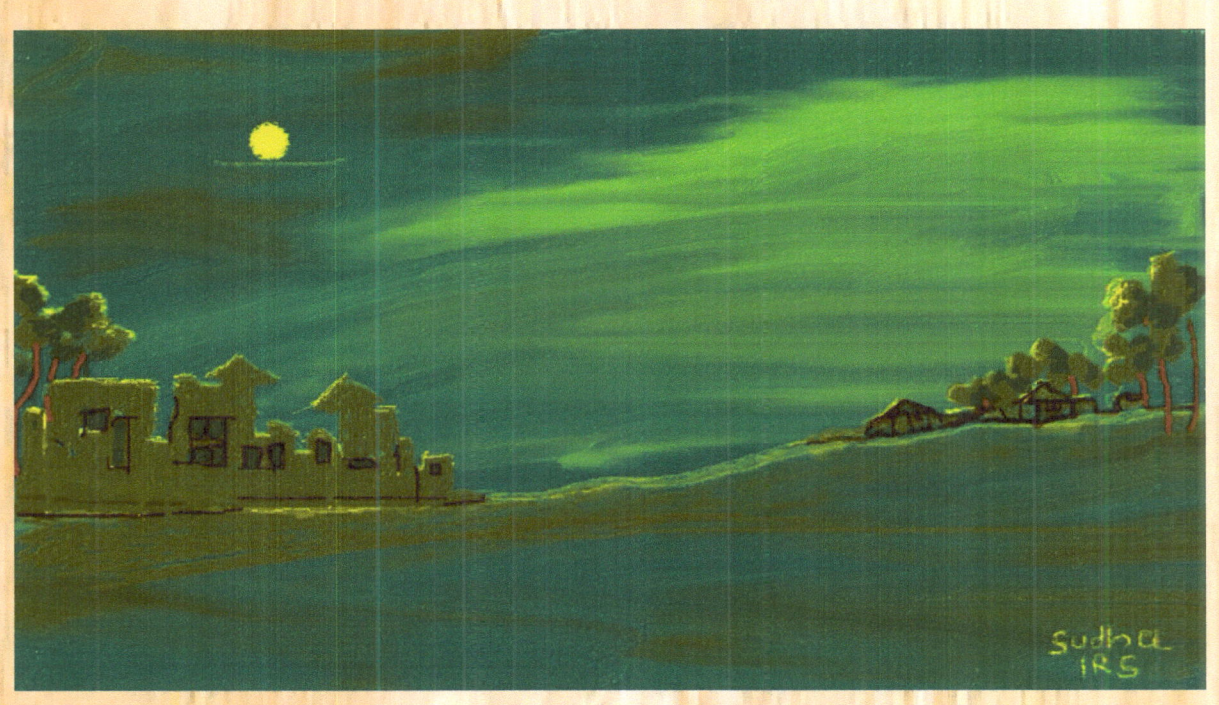

Yellow Moon on a Hamlet (digital graphics) 2016

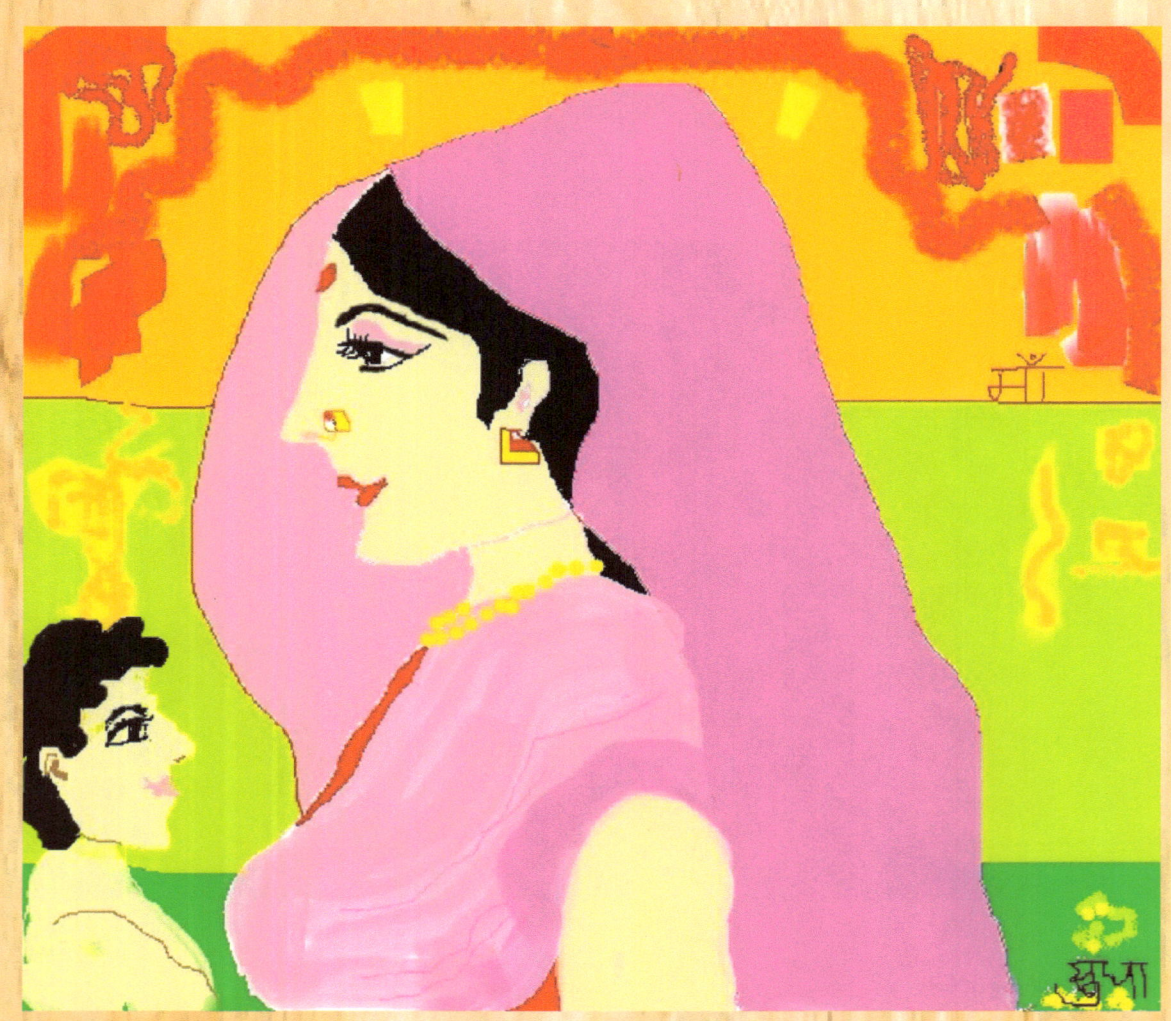

Mother (digital graphics) 2012

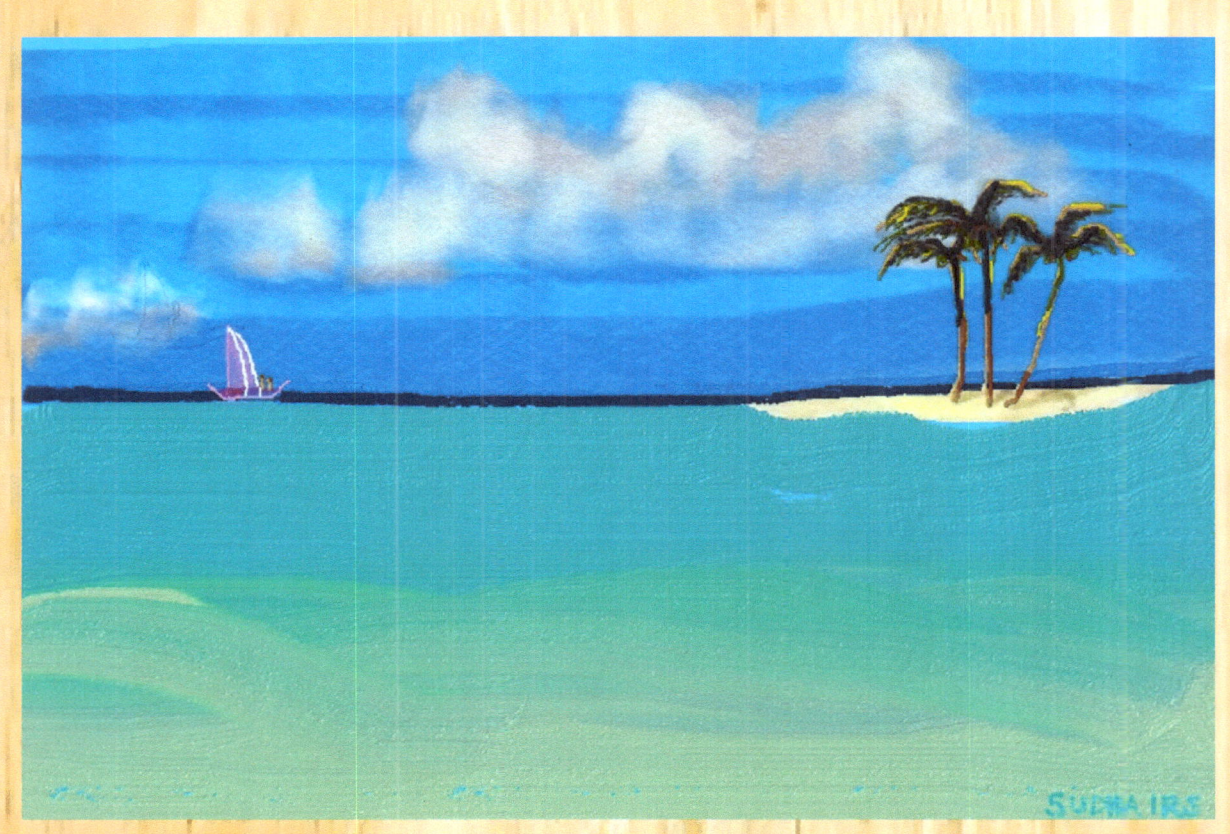

Sunlit Island (digital graphics) 2015

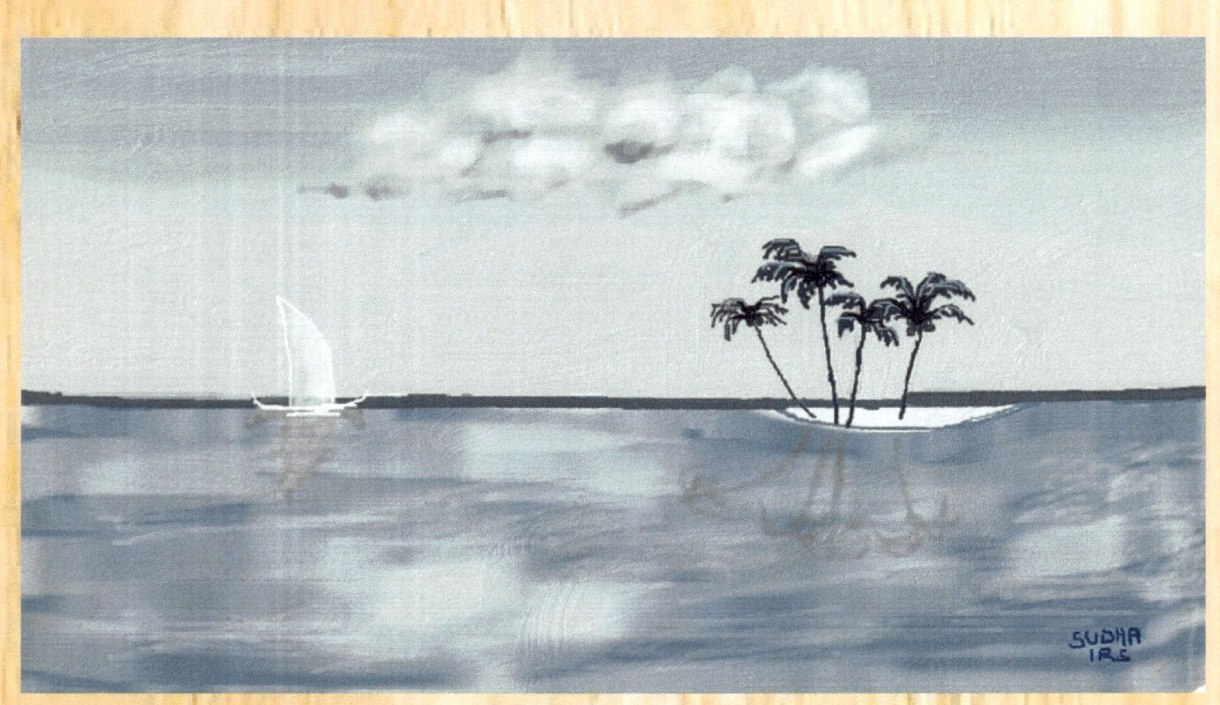

Island in Gray colour (digital graphics) 2015

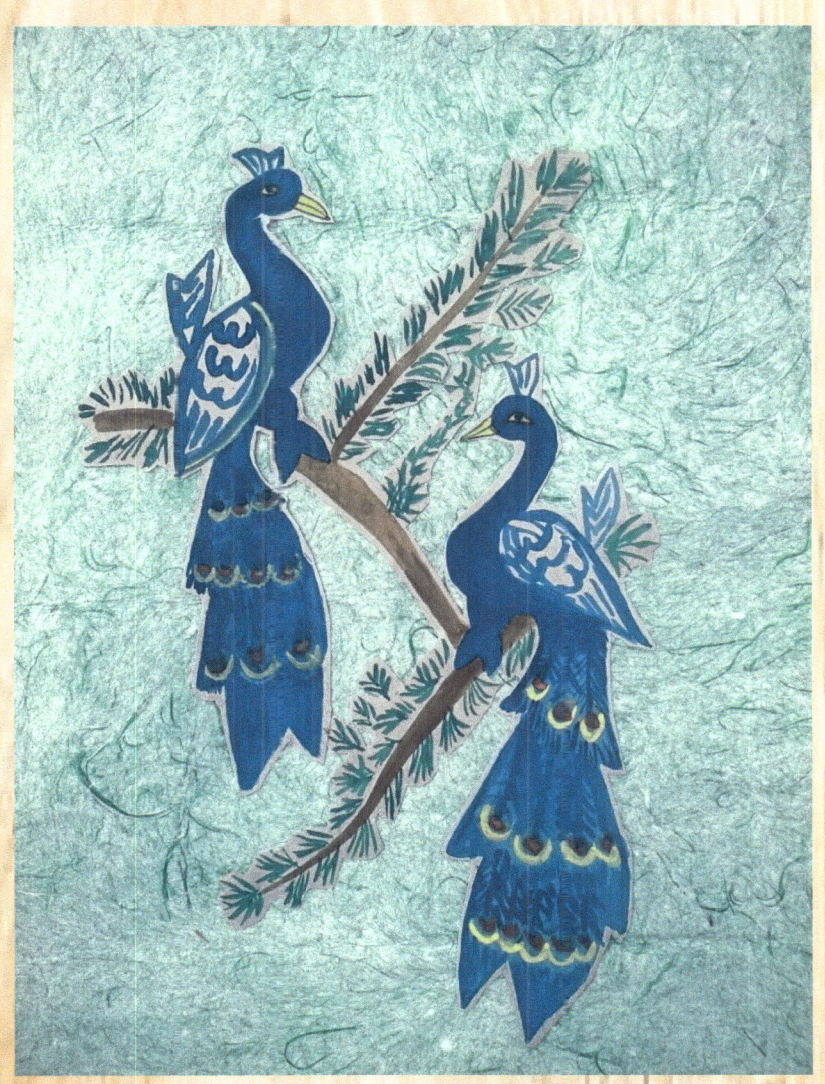

The Peacocks (water) 1978

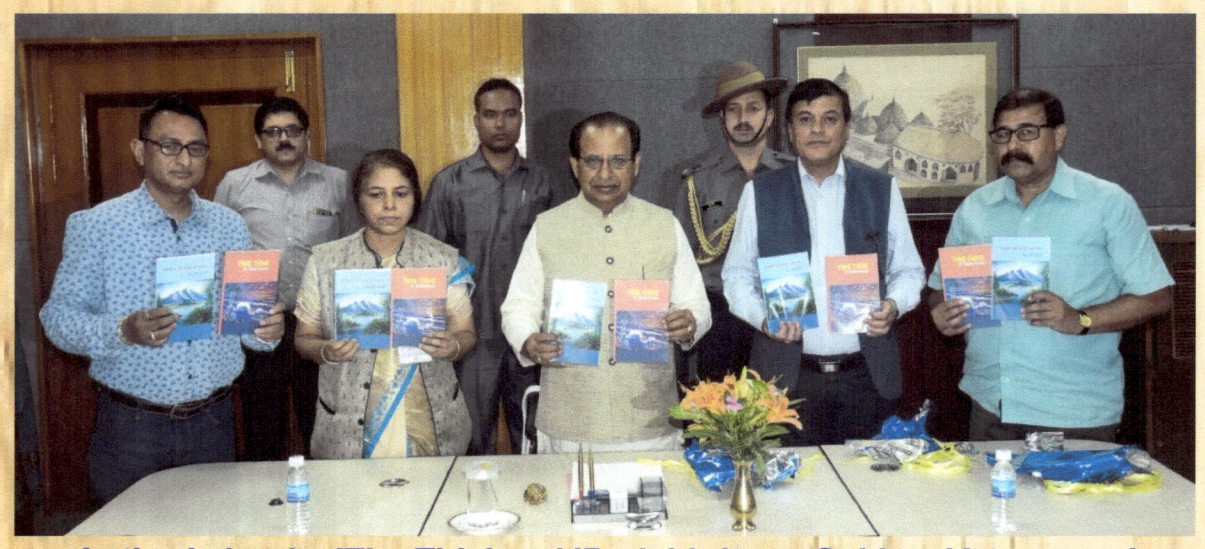

Author's books 'The Tide' and 'Parishkrit aur Sukhee Vataavaran' released by His Excellency the Governor of Assam at Guwahati.

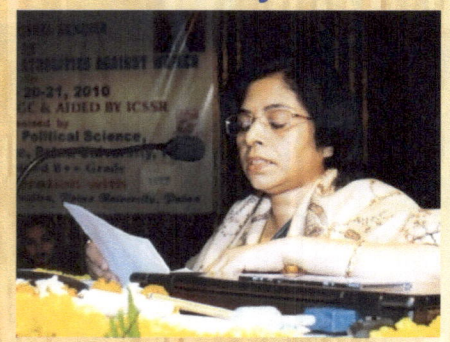
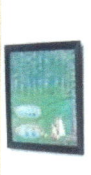
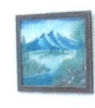
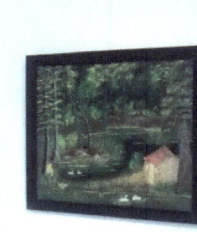
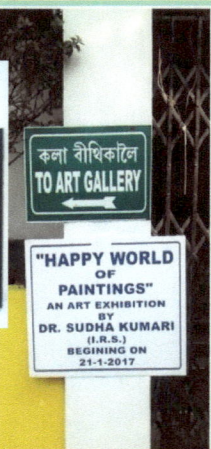

Author speaking at UGC Seminar at Patna

Author's art exhibition at Gallery Artists' Guild, Guwahati